LESS CLUTTER

A Life's Teachings

BARBARA HEMPHILL

Artwork and Photography by Louise Wannier

Published by True Roses, Inc.
in association with
www.LouiseWannier.com
www.BarbaraHemphill.com
888-380-6799

Hemphill, Barbara
Wannier, Louise

ISBN#: 978-0-9909976-0-3

© October 2014 by Barbara Hemphill with Artwork and Photography by Louise Wannier.

Printed in the USA by East Coast Digital Printing.

10   9   8   7   6   5   4   3   2

All rights reserved.

The following federally-registered trademarks and copyrights are
property of Barbara Hemphill:

• Less Clutter More Life© and Less Clutter™ (Jointly owned with Louise Wannier)
• Clutter is Postponed Decisions®
• Art of Wastebasketry®
• The Productive Environment Process™

All Photography, Artwork and Design Copyright Louise Wannier, LouiseWannier.com.
Cover art: Gentle Dream, Petal, Wisteria See

For Alfred and Michael

Blooms

Foreword

Clutter takes on many forms and has many consequences.

Lost papers.
Missing keys.
Late bills.
Wasted time.
Frustrated emotions.
Damaged relationships.

For too many people, clutter has become a standard of living. Our society has grown accustomed to filling up our homes, our cars, our offices, our calendars, and even our minds with much more "stuff" then we can manage. This pursuit often begins with the mindset that the more stuff we have or do, the more happiness we will experience. Sadly, many people find themselves in a place of discovering that the "pursuit of happiness" has cluttered up their lives so much that they are unable to enjoy the life that we were created and called to live.

Clutter often results from the development of habits. However, it is important to remember that habits are subject to our choices to change. Organization is a choice you can make to develop systems and skills to help you enjoy more freedom in your life. If this change is one that you desire to make then this is the book for you. The easy-to-follow wisdom of Barbara Hemphill will help motivate you to conquer the clutter in your home or office while guiding you through the processes and principles needed to help you make choices and changes that will enable you to experience less clutter and more life!

Christie Love,
Founder & Executive Director of LeadHer
(www.LeadHer.org)

Valentine

Life's Learnings.....

I attended school from kindergarten through eighth grade in a one-room schoolhouse in southeast Nebraska. I was a lanky blonde-headed girl with scaly skin and crooked legs. My classmates mockingly called me *Frosti*. If anyone would have told me then that I would grow up to become CEO of an international company, a best-selling author, and a speaker on the national circuit, I certainly would have laughed.

My family lived in three rooms on the top floor of a two-story farmhouse. What was the living room couch by day became two beds for my brother and me by night. My parents taught us how to use space wisely, and to think of the purpose of what every article had in our household. If it did not serve a function, it could not take up valuable real estate. Both my parents were entrepreneurial role models. On our dairy farm, my father adopted innovative ways of feeding cows and managing land. As an administrative assistant in the local bank, my mother gained the knowledge of farm management and used it to help my father realize his dreams. Working together, they developed strategies to manage their business to make it thrive, from big picture ideas of making the best use of their land resources to implementing systems for records management.

I struggled for years with what is now known as ADHD. As a result of repeated bullying, I attempted to end my life at age eleven. Thankfully my brother found me before I suffocated. The piano became my best friend. My mother said she could tell what kind of day I was having by the music I was playing when she came home from work.

Armed with my new realizations, I took seven dollars from the grocery money and put an ad in a local newspaper: "Organizing consultant can help you make better use of time and space." A year after I started offering residential organizing services, I went to the Small Business Administration to ask for their advice on how to grow what I now realized was a business. They laughed and said this was not a viable idea. They believed no one would pay for residential organizing service. Little did they know that residential organizing would grow to be a one billion dollar industry.

Within a few years, it became very clear to me that the biggest organizing challenge in the American home was paper. I wrote a book Taming the Paper Tiger which was excerpted world-wide in Reader's Digest. My hopes were dashed when the book publisher declared bankruptcy and distribution ceased. Then I had to borrow money to purchase back my literary rights. By persevering, I was able to have it re-released by Kiplinger's. I then focused my organizing practice on consulting with businesses. I taught business clients how to eliminate paper and physical clutter based on the principles I learned from my parents in those earlier years.

The dawning of the internet offered new opportunities for my business to expand in order to address digital clutter. I collaborated in the development of Taming the Paper Tiger software and helped promote it. I began training other women to become organizing consultants using the systems and strategies I developed.

My business was my life raft as I struggled with the aftermath of my first marriage. As I sat in a therapist's office, she asked, "What do you want? You have a clean slate." I answered, "I have no idea." She replied, "Let's start with what you don't want." Identifying what I didn't want clarified what I did want. That realization changed my life, and impacted the way I help individuals and organizations today.

Cherub

The transformation of Hemphill, Inc continued as I became acutely aware that there is a subtle kind of emotional and spiritual clutter which truly prevents people from accomplishing their work and enjoying their lives. It is my belief that God put each of us on this earth for a specific purpose. Unresolved issues cloud our ability to carry out our purpose, and become emotional clutter. Lack of clarity about our purpose can cause us to stumble through life and collect spiritual clutter.

Our lives are a puzzle, but unlike a puzzle that you and I might put together by completing the edges first, only God has the frame for our lives.

Grey Life

"And the Lord answered, behold he hath hid himself among the stuff"

- Samuel 10:22b (KJV)

Puzzle Bark

Life's a puzzle...
yet without an edge.

Life is a puzzle. We may not know or understand how it all fits together.
We may sometimes be fearful and uncertain.

Unlike a physical puzzle, where we *can* assemble the corners and put the border
pieces together first, our life's puzzle is ever-expanding.

Anything is possible and everything that happens is a piece in the puzzle.
Stay open and accept the possibilities your life offers.

Begin

State Your Vision:

Imagine the life you truly want.

How would you like to live your life?

What matters most to you?

There are no wrong answers, just choices. Describe the environment that nourishes you.

State Your Vision:

If you don't know what you want…

Start with what you don't want.

Eliminate the clutter that doesn't support the life you truly desire and what you need will emerge.

Identify your Obstacles:

Clutter is postponed decisions.®

Most of what we keep we never use, and ironically, the more we keep, the less we use.

Most lives are full of postponed decisions…..
Your closet may contain many examples.

What is in yours?

Is it expensive clothing you've never worn?

Perhaps the papers on the kitchen counter are a good example. Do you often pick up one, pause, consider, and then put it back down?

Or how about the email in your inbox? Do you open them, close them, open them, and then close them again?

Placid

Identify Your Obstacles:

What stops us?

- I never have enough time.
- I have too much to do.
- I have better things to do; organizing is boring.
- It's too difficult.
- It never lasts; it is never good enough.
- I often overthink the situation.
- I didn't create it; I have no idea what is there.
- I am easily distracted and go off on tangents.
- I get stuck in the memories of the past.
- It is too emotionally draining.
- I want to be responsible and respectful of things I have been given.
- I have to take care of other people and other things in my life first.
- It is hard to admit I have an issue.
- I am afraid to let something go; I might want it back.

Reflecting on these, what else would you add?

Stone

Deep emotional loss…

Every time I find someone who is having difficulty letting go, I keep asking questions until they realize the source. Here are a few I have heard:

"My mother died when I was six."

"I lost the job I loved."

"I always wanted to be a dancer, but this illness changed everything."

"My parents kept everything."

"I always wanted to be a mom."

"My husband left me ten years ago."

"We lost our child…"

…What else comes to mind?

Dream

Sharing Stories:

Start from where you are. You can't fix the past.

Linda had a room in her house that was full of clutter.

She dreaded going through all of it. Her "stuff" had become like a black hole; she didn't even know what was there anymore… a room full of papers, gifts, wrapping supplies, shopping bags and everything else you can imagine. Her clutter had become an unmanageable mass, too gigantic to even think about, let alone organize.

Her yearning for a peaceful place to meditate helped her let go of the past, start from where she was, and move toward where she wanted to be.

Sharing Stories:

The real issue is the trapped emotion.

Pat's five children had grown up and moved out of the family home, starting their adult lives elsewhere. Her home was full of their childhood belongings that they had left behind. She couldn't make the decisions of what was important for each of her children.

I sat down at Pat's computer and typed while she dictated a letter to each of the kids and gave them a specific amount of time to get their memorabilia, toys, school papers and collections out of her home.

Months later when the clutter was gone, Pat said, "I sleep better at night." The weight that was literally hanging over her head was gone.

Gentling

Bloom

Sharing Stories:

Twenty-three people in a non-profit office had offices and storage rooms filled with clutter.

To tackle the daunting, overwhelming task of creating a productive environment, we created an event. The morning began with everyone gathering in the conference room for a treat of bagels, fruit, and coffee followed by a seminar entitled, "Sometimes It Takes an Expert to Take Out the Trash!"

Following the seminar, we set up locations for "Trash to Treasure," recycling, and shredding around the office while the employees returned to start going through their desks, files, shelves, and storage rooms. We offered prizes to those who found the funniest thing, the oldest thing, and the most unlikely thing. The oldest thing was a 27-year-old receipt for 38 cents for a piece of hardware. The funniest thing was a petrified orange. At the end of the day, 3.5 tons of paper had been shredded!

Many participants were anxious to go home and continue the process. I heard several exclaim, "I feel lighter!"

Love Line

Reasons Given:

I need to do it myself.

- I don't want anyone to see my mess.
- These are my papers, these are my ideas.
- I have to do it all myself

When people realize that they don't have to do it all themselves, they feel relieved and hopeful.

Hydrangea

Reasons Given:

I can't let go.

"You just saved my marriage. I came to this seminar with the intention of telling my husband of 13 years I was leaving. I never understood before that it was not that he wouldn't let go of the clutter, but that he couldn't.

"You suggested saying: 'I never understood how important all this is to you. Let's figure out how to keep it.'

"Suddenly the dynamics changed.

"He felt heard. He felt that what he cared about really mattered. When he didn't feel like he had to hang on for dear life, he realized that he didn't need it all, and began letting go. In the process, he discovered what he really wanted."

A Note about Collections:

Whether related to your profession or your past times, collections often create clutter. They represent a huge investment of time, energy and money. Often you are passionate about them when you create them, but how often do you actually look at them now? Maybe simply taking a picture of the collection would suffice. How important is the collection? When was the last time you spent time with it? Has your passion for it waned? Maybe, simply taking a picture of the collection would suffice. Because it was valuable to you in the past doesn't necessarily mean it still is today.

Sharing Stories:

It isn't a moral issue; guilt isn't helpful.

It is your choice whether to keep your beloved mother's silver anniversary ring or give it away.

The costs of clutter are both emotional and financial. Clutter costs money to store, and makes it more difficult to find the things we care about. Clutter affects the environment in our homes, so that we enjoy them less. It reengages our brains repeatedly to remember stories of our past, often distracting or preventing us from moving on with our present lives.

In the end, if you can't find it, or don't remember you have it, it is clutter.

Your life reflects the decisions you make about your possessions and yourself.

Flutters

Reasons Given:

It's just too boring...

I haven't discovered anyone who is able to accomplish their work and enjoy their life who hasn't learned to overcome the stumbling block of boredom, but as the old saying goes, "If you keep doing what you're doing, you will keep experiencing what you have been having." Is that what you want? If not, think about things you can do to make the task at hand more pleasant:

Sing your favorite song or hum your favorite tune while you sort; Give yourself permission to let go and be silly, have a dance from pile to pile. Treat yourself to something you enjoy, maybe a manicure or a hot fudge sundae, when you're done;

Invite a friend to help you and take turns.
Give in to your inner child, have fun with it!

> *Linda has a 10-year old granddaughter who just loves to help, sorting all the makeup, beauty products, linens, and silver.*
>
> *Linda gets the reward of less clutter and quality time with someone she cares about.*

Sharing Stories:

Make your clutter someone else's blessing.

Jean's husband died 10 years ago…

"Every time I give away something of his, I am going to give away something of mine. Just think of how many people our things can now bless….. In 37 years of helping people, no one had yet said that… Her friend noted, "I have been friends with this woman for 10 years… I am so glad this has happened…"

Another piece of the puzzle…

Sharing Stories:

Does all of the clutter in the house belong to other family members?

I'm married to someone who isn't the least bit bothered by clutter, or if he is, he doesn't recognize it. When we were first married, I thought it was going to be the death of me. Then I realized the biggest way to relieve my stress was to focus on my own clutter and leave his alone — or at least keep it contained in specific parts of the house, which you can easily identify when you come to visit!

I decided a happy marriage was far more important.

Beach Spray

Reasons Given:

I hate to throw away useful things.

You don't have to throw away useful things,
and I encourage you not to, whenever possible
and practical.

Put a box in some easily accessible location on every
floor in your home. Choose a size that will be easy
to load in the car when it's full.

Label it clearly "Give away."

Whenever you find something you don't really want
or need, but someone else might, put it in the box.

Tell other family members about the boxes.
No need to nag them.

Just start the practice yourself —
and see what happens.

Ripple

Reasons Given:

I don't have time to clear the clutter.

Clearing the clutter from your house doesn't have to be a big project. Set aside at least one hour each week to clear the clutter from one small area at a time.

...Skip a TV show?

....Make a date with yourself?

Helpful Tips

Be sure to allow ten minutes at the end of each hour to clean up.
- Get rid of the trash.
- Move items you find that belong elsewhere to their right places (even if you have to temporarily "stash them").
- Put the items that others can use in a *give away* box.
- Have a plan for how, when and where they need to go.

Sharing Stories:

Sometimes, it is just life's circumstances…

A number of years ago I was hired by a woman — a high school principal and a naturally organized person — who suddenly needed to care for her aging parents and her sick husband. Very quickly, the mail, unread magazines and other forms of clutter in her household started to accumulate.

When she could no longer stand the disorganization, she hired me.

When we were done, she gave a party. She even put candles in the laundry room. She wanted everyone to see that the paper clutter that had been scattered around the house was really gone, and she hadn't hidden it in laundry baskets as she had been doing for several years.

Begin From Where You Are:

Any progress will move you forward…

Let go of thinking of everything that has to be done — simply take the next step.

Instead of asking "What should I do?"

ask yourself,

"What am I able to do?"

Begin with a single change.

Erica decided she would give up her daily stop at the coffee shop, and instead make coffee at home. With the money she saved, she hired a service to organize her expense receipts.

Be gentle.

Pace yourself.

Design & Execute the Plan: Make the Choices

If you want a golden rule that will eliminate clutter, this is it:

> Have nothing in your houses that you do not know to be useful or believe to be beautiful."
>
> *— William Morris*

Your best decisions are based on love and hope, not fear.

Love

Design & Execute the Plan: Make the Choices

Ask yourself...

Does ***this*** item (thought or feeling)
help me to accomplish my work or enjoy my life?

If your answer is no,

it is clutter.

Peach Rose

Sharing Stories:

A client of mine who is an artist lived in a very dark and cluttered house. She told me she dreamed of a white tower with lots of glass. I responded, "It seems your spirit is longing to be free."

We started with her closet. I will never forget the look on her face when I asked, "How does looking at this dress make you feel?" I added, "If you feel fat, ugly, guilty, depressed, or anything negative when you look at it, you can't afford to keep it." She amazed me, as she started packing up clothes for donation, her energy rising with every decision until she had space for her new life.

"Creativity is a messy process — things often get worse before they get better."

Design & Execute the Plan: Make the Choices

How does this item (or thought) make me feel?

Letting go inspires hope.

We often have emotional and spiritual attachments to our belongings.

If the item, or the thought when you look at the item, causes negative emotions, pause and breathe, consider your thoughts, and ask yourself what does this item really mean to you? What do you notice?

Sometimes we are surprised by what arises when we ask.

Do you feel responsible or guilty? Was it given to you by someone you loved? Did it cost a lot of money? Did it take a long time to make?

Letting go of clutter increases simplicity.

Sharing Stories:

Create a space so that new things can appear.

When I returned from living in India, I brought the beautiful grand piano I had purchased there with the money I inherited from my grandmother. It was an exquisite instrument. The mechanism was made in France, and was the same kind that Chopin played on; the case was hand-made in India of solid teakwood.

Years later, however, the sounding board was cracked and the mechanism beyond repair. I gave it away — creating a space. I had to give up that Pleyel piano in order to have the far finer Petrof piano I enjoy playing today.

Often, we have to end one relationship before we can begin another, and in between, make peace with ourselves and our situation.

Clear Field

"We can't solve problems by using the same kind of thinking we used when we created them."

- *Albert Einstein*

Curly Life

Design and Execute the Plan: Make the Choices

Create a system for anything done repeatedly.

A SYSTEM is a practice that Saves You Space, Time, Energy and Money.

What do you do repeatedly?

You repeatedly do many things: the laundry, open the mail, pay bills, eat, exercise, work, run errands, do housework, study, and many more. What do you do repeatedly in your life?

For each of these, you need a system.

The system enables you to keep track of what is important to you and to live your life with greater ease.

Together

Design and Execute the Plan: Make the Choices

A good system to handle paper.

I have found that for most people (even those committed to moving toward digital), paper is the most challenging organizing issue and the hardest to face.

Creating a system you can use for paper you want or need to keep provides the foundation for organizing the rest of your life. All of your relationships will benefit, productivity will increase, and peace of mind will be more attainable.

Start organizing your papers by sorting them into big categories first:

- Put like things together.
- Create subcategories only when the big categories become unmanageable.

Design and Execute the Plan: Make the Choices

For each piece of paper, choose one of these three:

FILE only when you think you may still need it and don't feel you can throw it away. (Keep as much as you wish, but as little as possible since you remember the cost of saving it)

ACT when the ball is in your court, what is the next action? By when?

TOSS (delete or recycle) whenever possible; means you don't need it!

Ingenue

Clear Peak

Sharing Stories:

Out of the cluttered front-hall closet in the home of a former ambassador came the "Home Office for the Business of Life™ — a place where she paid bills, dealt with social schedules, managed consumer issues, and corresponded with friends. What made it work was the radio we put there where she could listen to her favorite program while accomplishing her work.

The owner observed, "If I had done this 20 years ago, life would have been so much easier and much more pleasant!"

Every home needs a command central.

Remember to choose a place you enjoy.

Design and Execute the Plan: Evaluate

Is it the right system for me?

Take a moment and review these four questions:

- Does the system work?
- Do you like the system?
- Does it work for others?
- Can you recover quickly from life's inevitable messes?

If the answer to any of these questions is "No," tweak and make adjustments until your system is right for you.

For example, for time and project management, I use a paper planner along with my digital calendar. One of the things that makes the difference between this system working and not working is keeping my paper planner open, so I can write immediately on it whenever possible, instead of having to re-write notes.

Be mindful of a common block: perfectionism. Rethinking and redoing systems is often an unproductive time waster. Does it really have to be perfect?

"Now I just do it until it works well enough. What used to take me months now only takes me two weeks."

Clarity

Growth

Sharing Stories:

Making space refuels your life…

John spent thousands of dollars and thousands of hours on advanced degrees as he built his first career. Later, he went from being a high-powered lawyer to becoming a mentor for at-risk boys. He no longer needed any of the books and notes from the past. He was reluctant to let them go. He felt like he was throwing away a part of himself.

He realized, however, that he could let go of what he no longer needed in order to fully embrace his new life passion.

Pure Rose

Sharing Stories:

A new path or "just in case"…

Andrea used to be a teacher so she kept everything she might need in case she decided to teach again. Keeping things "just in case" is emotionally admitting that you are not sure you are going to succeed. After consideration, she was able to release the materials and is now secure and growing in her new profession.

Photographs from other people's families are difficult to release, particularly if you received them from your best friend. Instead of telling yourself you are being uncaring, release them. In their place, take time to put the names and ages of your friends' children in your contacts so when you next talk you will have them.

Files can also be fun! I love to take day trips with a friend or family member. A file called "Adventure Possibilities" is a file where I store ideas for such a day. A client created a "Warm Fuzzy" file — a place she put papers that brought happy memories for those inevitable days when everything seemed to be going wrong.

Sharing Stories:

The president of a company worked with one of our certified productivity consultants as his coach to establish his new plan and system.

His miracle happened in just six hours. Now he texts his coach every week to say, "See, the system is still working!"

Before

After

Wave Spray 2

Reinforcement:

Don't skip the ten minutes!

At the end of each hour's sorting, physically take eliminate: — (move) — doesn't add anything — items to wherever they need to be. If that place is not organized, it's a project for another day!

That way, the things you have put aside won't return to the closet, and you won't have to go through the process all over again.

Be sure not to skip the ten minutes at the end of each hour's sorting.

Emotional Clutter:

Often you have to give up "great" to get the "best."

You can have anything you want, though not everything.
A little shift can make a huge difference.

"My favorite food in the world is ice cream. I want to eat it when I am celebrating, when I am lonely, and especially when I am sad.

But after many years of struggle, I know that if I do, I will sacrifice the energy I crave for my physical body.

*Now I **choose** to have it…sometimes…"*

Fireworks

Solo Spray 2

Sustain your Success:

Allow for expansion — new 'stuff' is continually arriving.

From time to time, review your systems. Go back and look at what's working and what isn't.

Consider whether anything significant has changed since you last evaluated the system, and review the four questions again:

- Does it still work?
- Do you still like it?
- Is it working for others?
- Can you recover quickly from life's inevitable messes?

Has there been an unanticipated obstacle? Your health affects organizing quite a bit. Is your desk chair the culprit? When you hurt physically you can't do what you intend. So, care for yourself and get a new chair. Adjust your ergonomics until you are comfortable in your work and your life.

Are you filing more than you need to keep?

> *…One day we found dollar bills someone neatly filed…*

Self

Sustain your Success:

What legacy do you wish to leave those you love?

Are you accomplishing your work and enjoying your life?

Sustain your Success:

Together we are better…

Holding yourself accountable while making changes is easier when other people are there to guide and support you.

"First I figure out what I do best, I do that, and then I pass along what is best done by the other, so we each do our best."

Twins

Exodus 17:12

So it came about when Moses held his hand up, that Israel prevailed, and when he let his hand down, Amalek prevailed.

But Moses' hands were heavy. Then they took a stone and put it under him, and he sat on it; and Aaron and Hur supported his hands, one on one side and one on the other. Thus his hands were steady until the sun set.

"Change is a permanent condition of a healthy individual and a healthy organization."

— Barbara Hemphill

Barbara's hair and make-up by Melissa Naron
Barbara's photograph by Brandi Autry
Barbara's clothing and scarf design by Louise Wannier (LouisJane.com)

For as long as I can remember I longed to experience peace. My grandfather once said that if you didn't hear God, it was because you had "skeletons in your closet," so at a subconscious level, perhaps my search for God led me to be an organizing consultant and ultimately to the peace I experience today. My hope is that this book will contribute to your ability to create and sustain an environment in which you can accomplish your work and enjoy your life.

It is a lifelong process, so never give up!

Camelia Cream

Where to go for help

For more information about how to do what you have decided to do, go to www.LessClutterMoreLife.com for additional resources.

If you need help, find someone whom you trust, someone who has proven experience, and someone who respects that the decisions are yours alone. If you want professional help, contact Productive Environment Institute (www.ProductiveEnvironment.com).

Productive Environment Institute (PEI) evolved from Barbara Hemphill Associates which was founded in 1978. PEI's mission is to offer training and support for individuals, largely women, who want a career in which they can put their family first, and have meaningful work with substantial income opportunities and flexible hours. Today, PEI includes a growing international team of Certified Productive Environment Specialists (CPESs) whose mission is helping individuals manage time, space, and information — ultimately transforming how they live and work — and helping organizations increase profit, productivity, and peace of mind. (www.BecomeASpecialist.com)

www.ProductiveEnvironment.com
Hemphill & Associates, Inc./Productive Environment Institute
467 Lake Eva Marie Drive Raleigh,
North Carolina 27603 United States
(888) 380-6799

Trust the process....
gently begin, invite a friend.

If you want someone to help you, find someone whom you trust, someone who has proven experience, and someone who respects that the decisions are yours alone.

Sharing Stories: Louise's Note

While working with Barbara on this book, we both realized that I needed to experience her teachings directly.

My jewelry drawer had been a mess for more than ten years and it had been on my "to do" list for the same amount of time; I was stuck.

"Come on, let's just start…", said Barbara.

One by one, I took everything out of the drawer, and Barbara stood at my side gently guiding. It takes energy to stand and face the choices. Is this one to keep, make someone a present of, or simply give away?

"Will I ever wear this again, do I need it to remember the time I received it, does it bring to mind the memory of the past dear?"

I silently asked myself these questions as we took out each item, stopping for a moment to recall, treasure, and then pass along to Barbara, who was gently organizing the piles on the bed as I made each decision. Thank you from the bottom of my heart, dear one. I felt such a release and arising joy from being able to simply see and enjoy the jewels from my memories that I want to enjoy and keep.

Here are the categories resulting from sorting my jewelry drawer:

- Keep in the drawer: necklaces, bracelets, earrings
- Mend / Polish
- Give away
- Gift, bless someone new
- Buttons and thread (put with my sewing)
- Toss / Trash
- Mementoes (file somewhere else)

See the difference! (shown below: from Chaos came Clarity…)

Before   *After*

Synthesis:

In summary, here are the 5 steps: Follow each in turn and keep number 5 for life...

1. State *your* vision
2. Identify *your* obstacles
3. Commit *your* resources
4. Design and execute *your* plan
5. Sustain *your* success

Acknowledgements:

This book would not have been possible....

Frequently a consulting company is named "… & Associates" to imply that the company is larger than it may actually be. In truth, that was my intent when I incorporated 35+ years ago.

So many people have helped me on this journey. My family have been continuously supportive even when my efforts seemed ridiculous; my friends from around the world have provided encouragement and expertise when I needed it most — especially my lifelong friend, Florence Feldman, to whom I said, "I could do this if someone would just believe in me." My business coaches and colleagues have been role-models of success in their own lives and businesses. The Toss/Trash Mementoes from the Certified Productive Environment Specialist community who promote the principles in this book, have been of deep emotional support. My business partner, Andrea Anderson, without whom there would be no Productive Environment Institute, and Louise Wannier who made my dream of writing a book that would be my legacy come true, have been true friends and colleagues.

White Rose

Thank you so much to the brave family, friends and clients who have encouraged us to share their stories and have read through numerous drafts and given their honest and frank feedback. They have added the human touch.

Thanks to our publishing support team: Kat Ward and Florence Feldman for their brilliant editing. Kat helped us particularly to elucidate the motivation behind each story and Flo helped me to remember the most important stories and to use the best words to represent each teaching. Jeni Kozicky (AbstractHabitat.com) is a terrific graphic designer who helped to resolve the final details in the layout. Cailin Traum, Louise's patient, diligent and resourceful assistant helped us in so many ways.

A deep thank you again to our husbands, Alfred and Michael, for their love, support and care of each of us. To Alfred, especially, I am continually blessed by your commitment to "block and tackle" so I can fly.

Wise Eyes

Afterword

Barbara and I each faced a block when beginning to create this book together. For Barbara it was the block of needing the right kind of collaborator. "I can't just go lock myself up and write this. I can't do it alone. This is not a 'how to' book. It is a 'why to' book, which means that I have to capture emotions, and emotions require the presence of art." For Louise, it was the first time bringing her artistic work to a conclusion that would sufficiently support the goal: "I faced the block as an artist of self-inflicted repression. Would it be good enough to enliven Barbara's life's work sufficiently well to inspire those who read it?" Our hope is that this book brings you further inspiration to "accomplish your work and enjoy your life" to its fullest, as the journey of creating it has done for each of us.

Warm regards,

Barbara and Louise

September 22, 2014

If you enjoyed this one, look for the next one, coming in 2015: *Less Clutter More Health*

Testimonials

"In the process of decluttering your environment, sooner or later you will uncover your real Self. This simple yet profound work Barbara put together serves as a guiding light for the process of clearing the way to the life you deeply desire. After so many passionate years of teaching others how to get organized, she shares heart-warming stories of transformation that each have a way of touching your heart and soul. It is both a beautiful and empowering experience."

Ericka D. Jackson, Master Business and Ministry Trainer, President, The Convergence Center LLC.

"What keeps you from enjoying more life — dark, runaway thoughts? Broken systems? Encapsulated emotions? Barbara Hemphill and Louise Wannier engage you in this book with bright, positive stories, improved processes, and beautiful images which release more life from within you. Less Clutter, More Life will never clutter and instead helps create a more and better life for you."

Dr. Joey Faucette, Speaker, Coach, & Best-Selling Author of Work Positive in a Negative World

"**Less Clutter More Life** brings new clarity to how emotional and spiritual clutter prevents you from getting the most out of life. A great read to help unlock the why behind the clutter which will bring more purpose, success and happiness to your Life!"

Tom Popow, President, Sunset Ridge Chiropractic

"Do you long to experience renewed energy, fresh joy, incredible freedom? Then open these amazing pages and be revived, transformed, enlivened and enlightened! What a gift you have given us, Barbara!"

Glenna Salsbury, Professional Speaker, Author of The Art of the Fresh Start

"I used to be overwhelmed by the time it would take to de-clutter anything in my life. Just thinking of the process and not having enough time to get it done, would literally make my head hurt. However, I've learned a focused approach of de-cluttering one thing in a set block of scheduled time. This principle has helped me tremendously in living a much more organized and peaceful life".

Antonina D. Geer, Co-Founder, Kingdom Driven Entrepreneur (Excerpt from Overwhelm to Peace)

"Barbara Hemphill is the author of books on decluttering and organizing -- something a recovering perfectionist like me has always devoured. One day in 2012, I followed a link on Barbara's newsletter, filled out a questionnaire, and she called me to discuss the results. I signed up for her "8-Hour Miracle," and ended up spreading the hours out over a long time because I injured my back and couldn't sit, let alone declutter "stuff." Rather than focusing on file drawers, as I'd expected, she got me to focus on the purpose of my life and to declutter my mind from all that was distracting me from finishing the book God had told me (through my dreams) to write. My life is so enriched as a result: Not only is my book now published, but I am expressing myself creatively every day, living my calling, and helping others to do the same!"

Chris Smith, Quilter, Christian Creativity Coach, and Author of Reap As You Sew

"As a fellow board member of ezeGlide Rollout Shelving, Barbra Hemphill has assisted us in designing products that create a more efficient, productive environment in the home or office. Barbara's innovative ideas on how to be better organized and more productive in our lives is life changing. Two words come to my mind when I think of Barbara Hemphill — 'Life Changer!'"

Patrick Kennedy, President and Founder of ezeGlide Inc.

Testimonials

"WOW! How wonderfully beautiful it is! The illustrations, simplicity, quotes, experiences…all help to capture a feeling of hope and that little nudge we all need. It's like a whisper of encouragement that yes, you too can tackle what is overcoming you. I've come to learn that the reasons my clients have clutter come in all different ways and reasons. Whether it's from loss and they haven't finished grieving, perhaps they didn't have much in their childhood, loneliness, depression & overwhelmed, delayed projects — "somedays", one thing is the same: it's emotional clutter. It's like dozens of piles of emotions everywhere. This book will help!"

Devon Broughton, Broker-Owner, Broughton Agency, Inc.

"This book is gorgeous. It somehow unclutters the mind and inspires the physical clearing that I needed. The beauty of this little book is the kind messages to people like me who are "guilty as charged." Just reading the tips (start from where you are, make your clutter someone else's blessing) and seeing the gorgeous photos is a sensory journey that I want to share over and over with friends."

Patty DeDominic, Entrepreneur, Founder International Women's Festivals,
President Emeritus National Association of Women Business Owners

"I've known Barbara Hemphill for more than 15 years and she never ceases to amaze me! In this book you will find two of Barbara's greatest passions in life — her passion for productivity, and perhaps more importantly, her passion for helping people. I'm grateful to be one of the people that Barbara has helped both personally and professionally, and when you read this book, you can be one too."

Joe Polish, Founder, Piranha Marketing and Genius Network, Co-founder of 10XTalk.com
and ILoveMarketing.com

"As the founder of a fitness & lifestyle training center built on Barbara Hemphill's teachings, I can tell you first hand about the power of the concepts in this book. My clients have transformed their bodies, their schedules, their homes and even their relationships by following Barbara's principles. This book will change you."

Demetrius Farrior, Founder, Demetrius Farrior's Island Training (DFIT)

"What Barbara Hemphill has done with *Less Clutter More Life* is simply incredible! She's created an amazing blueprint to help others experience more joy in life by becoming more focused on clearing all cutter that prevents them from getting the best that life has to give should be herald and actioned consistently. The simplicity of her strategies are masterful and exude her wealth of knowledge and expertise in this area. I am so grateful that Barbara wrote this book and I know that many lives will be changed upon reading it."

Darnyelle A. Jervey, CEO Incredible One Enterprises, LLC

"Barbara makes organization an art--a graceful and soulful experience! Her words not only inspire us to clean out the closet, they enthusiastically and gently encourage us to de-clutter our lives. Wonderful!"

Mary Knackstedt, Founder, Knackstedt, Inc. and author of The Interior Design Business Handbook.

"Barbara Hemphill is a beautiful blessing to all who listen. She helped transform my life with her simple yet powerful formula to conquer clutter. *Less Clutter More Life* is Barbara's crowning achievement as a writer and lifestyle pioneer. I love the feel and spirit of this book."

Bill Leslie, WRAL TV Anchor/Reporter

Testimonials

"This book is wonderful! I read it twice and decided to finally just get started on this clutter I have created in my life. You have motivated me to clean out and get organized and be free of the constant little voice in my head nagging me to just do it. Looking forward to all the free time I will have. Look out! My clutter is coming to an end!!"

Sally Kuykendoll, Owner, Curves, Garner, NC

"Businesspeople want to streamline their work and avoid the delays inherent with not being able to get their hands on information quickly. In addition, being disorganized causes a subtle form of constant mental fatigue that can sap creativity. "Yes", you are saying, "but who has the time to do maintenance when you are already running so hard?" Barbara knows the 'shortcuts' to really improving your speed, efficiency and joy in how you work. She does this in a format that is easy to learn and is packed full of the knowledge that only a true expert can deliver in a short read. This book is worth your time."

Jim Grady, Founder & CEO, The Paper Tiger Software

"In the face of the daunting task of "uncluttering" our lives, Barbara Hemphill shows us the way to let go, emotionally, spiritually and physically. Any business or individual seeking a more productive environment can achieve this with the guidance and tools offered by Barbara Hemphill in "Less Clutter, More Life".... simple, clear, guilt free and choice laden in ways that lead us to become more efficient and effective in our work space and in our personal life. What a gift!"

Jeanne Tedrow, Founder, Passage Home

"Barbara's approach is comprehensive and vital whether for you as an individual, or in our case for our company, from which we eliminated over 16 tons of paper and nearly half of the files from our servers prior to moving our offices."

Thomas Henning, President & CEO Assurity Life

"***Less Clutter, More Life*** takes us on an insightful journey of self-discovery. As Barbara guides readers through the physical, emotional and spiritual challenges that can be obstacles to the realization of a dream, Louise's magnificent photography inspires us to take a moment and appreciate the natural beauty of the world around us."

Maureen E. Ford Co-Author, Life Moments for Women, 108 Extraordinary California Women Share Turning Points in Their Lives